you make the

WORLD
BETTER

written by jennifer pletsch and m.h. clark • designed by jill labieniec

We live in a world filled with wonderful things—

with city lights and favorite places, with fantastic opportunities, grand surprises, and plenty of special moments in between. But these aren't the only things that make our world a delight. And they aren't the only things that make life rich. Because what really brings these wondrous things to life are the people we know—the ones who make the adventure worth taking, the ones who turn experiences into memories, the ones who make the world better.

You're one of those people. You add joy, humor, and meaning. You turn regular days into a celebration. And you can always be counted on to do something, no matter how simple it may seem, that will add extra to the ordinary.

Thanks for being you. Thanks for all the things you do. You make the world

Those who bring

SUNS

to the lives of other

HINE

annot keep it from themselves.

j. m. barrie

You are a

LIGHT.

...we make a life by what we

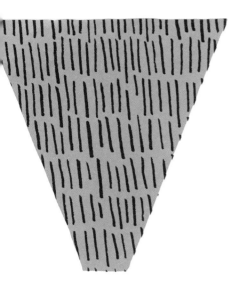

winston churchill

You add joy to

EVERY

day.

Go out into the world and do good until there i

oo much good in the

R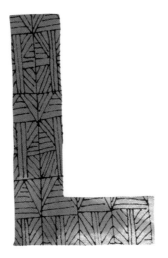L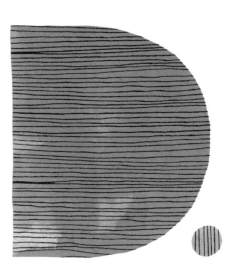D.

larry h. miller

You make life

SWEETER.

Blessed are those who can give without

REMEM

BERING

and take without forgetting.

elizabeth bibesco

You are an
INSPIRATION.

By being yourself, you put something

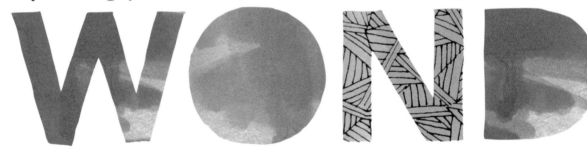

ERFUL

in the world that was not there before.

edwin elliot

You add extra to the

ORDINARY.

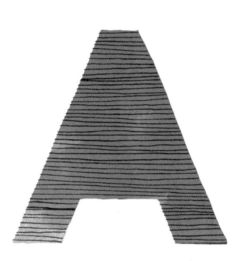 

IND

word is like a spring day.

russian proverb

You make each day more

BEAUTIFUL.

Your thoughts, words and deeds are

PAIN

TING

the world around you.

jewel diamond taylor

You are a

MARVEL.

Spread

wherever you go...

mother teresa

You add HEART to all you do.

What a difference one

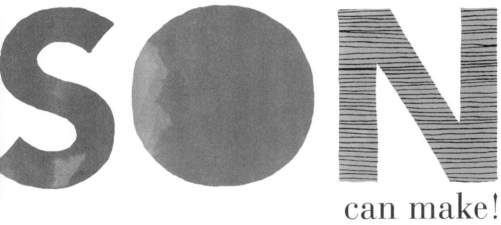

SON

can make!

sasha azevedo

You are one-of-a-kind
WONDERFUL.

Act your

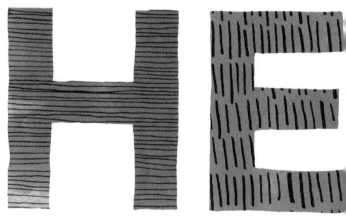

ART.

There's nothing else.

theodore roethke

You always

ADD JOY.

May  HAPP

touch your life today as warml

INESS

...s you have touched the lives of others.

rebecca forsythe

You bring out the best in

Some people look for a beautiful place. Other

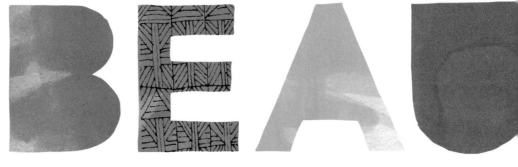

make a place

TIFUL.

inayat khan

You change things for the

BETTER.

ach day with light and heart.

john tillotson

You create a brighter

WORLD.

COMPENDIUM
live inspired.

With special thanks to the entire compendium family.

CREDITS:
Written by: Jennifer Pletsch and M.H. Clark
Designed by: Jill Labieniec
Edited by: Amelia Riedler
Creative Direction by: Julie Flahiff

ISBN: 978-1-938298-27-1

2nd printing. Printed in China with soy inks.